ANIMAL TRACKS
of Southern California

by Chris Stall

THE
MOUNTAINEERS

To D. C. V.; to M. C. M. C.; and to Bill & Iris.

The Mountaineers: Organized 1906 ". . . to explore, study, preserve, and enjoy the natural beauty of the outdoors."

First edition: first printing 1990,
Second printing 1997

Published by The Mountaineers
1001 SW Klickitat Way, Suite 201, Seattle, Washington 98134

Manufactured in the United States of America

Book design by Elizabeth Watson
Cover design by Nick Gregoric
Track on cover: Long-tailed Weasel

Library of Congress Cataloging in Publication Data
Stall, Chris.
     Animal tracks of southern California / by Chris Stall.
         p.   cm.
     Includes bibliographical references (p.   ).
     Includes index.
     ISBN 0-89886-237-X
     1. Animal tracks--California.   2. Mammals--California.   3. Birds--
California.   I. Title.
QL719.C2A55   1990
599.09794'9--dc20
                                         90-44019
                                            CIP

Contents

Preface

Most people don't get a chance to observe animals in the wild, with the exceptions of road kills and a few nearly tame species in parks and campgrounds. Many wild animals are nocturnal or scarce, and many are shy and secretive to avoid the attention of predators, or stealthy as they stalk their next meal. In addition, most wild creatures are extremely wary of humans either instinctively or because they've learned through experience to be that way. We may catch fortuitous glimpses now and then, but few of us have the time or motivation required for lengthy journeys into wild country for the sole purpose of locating animals. The result is that areas where we would expect to see animals often seem practically devoid of wildlife.

That's rarely the case, of course. Actually, many animals reside in or pass through all reasonably wild habitats. Though we may not see them, they nevertheless leave indications of their passage. But for the most part such signs are obscure or confusing so that only the most experienced and knowledgeable wilderness travelers notice them.

There's one grand exception: *animal tracks*. Often readily apparent even to the most casual and inexperienced observer, tracks not only indicate the presence of wild animals but can also be matched relatively easily with the animals that made them. I guess that's why I have been fascinated by animal tracks since my childhood in rural New York, and why that focus has continued through two decades of wandering and searching for them in wildlands all across North America.

Animal Tracks of Southern California is a compilation of many years and many miles of my own field work, protracted observations, sketching, photography, and research into articles and books too numerous to list and too heavy to carry into the backcountry.

Animal tracks may be something you concern yourself with only when you happen on them, or your interest in tracks may become nearly obsessive. You may find yourself hiking with your chin resting securely on your chest, feverishly scanning the ground for clues. You may seek out snow because tracks show up on it better than most other surfaces. In the absence of snow, you might find yourself altering your routes, avoiding bedrock and ground cover, seeking out damp sand, soft dirt, and mud along streams, near ponds and lakes, around swamps. You may journey into the desert in the early morning, before the sand dries and moves on the wind. After a rainfall, you might make special trips to check fresh mud, even along dirt roads or hiking trails, knowing that among evidence of human activity the animal prints will be clear and precise.

Whatever your degree of interest, I hope you will enjoy using this book, in your backyard or in the wildest and most remote regions of Southern California, and that your interest in identifying tracks grows until you reach the level of knowledge at which you no longer need this book.

Good luck!

Chris Stall
Cincinnati, Ohio

Introduction

HOW TO USE THIS BOOK

1. When you first locate an unknown track, look around the immediate area to locate the clearest imprint (see Tracking Tips below). You can usually find at least one imprint or even a partial print distinct enough for counting toes, noting the shape of the heel pad, determining the presence or absence of claw marks, and so on.

2. Decide what kind of animal is most likely to have made the tracks; then turn to one of the two main sections of this book. The first and largest features mammals; the second, much shorter section is devoted entirely to birds.

3. Measure an individual track, using the ruler printed on the back cover of this book. Tracks of roughly 5 inches or less are illustrated life-size; those larger than 5 inches have been reduced as necessary to fit on the pages.

4. Flip quickly through the appropriate section until you find tracks that are about the same *size* as your mystery tracks. The tracks are arranged roughly by size from smallest to largest.

5. Search carefully for the tracks in the size range that, as closely as possible, match the *shape* of the unknown tracks.

6. If you find the right shape, but the size depicted in the book is too big, remember that the illustrations represent tracks of an average *adult* animal. Perhaps your specimen was made by a young animal. Search some more; on the ground nearby you might locate the tracks of a parent, which will more closely match the size of the illustration.

7. Read the comments on range, habitat, and behavior to help confirm the identification.

This book is intended to assist you in making field identifications of commonly encountered animal tracks. To keep the book compact, my remarks are limited to each animal's most obvious characteristics. By all means enhance your own knowledge of these track makers. Libraries and book stores are good places to begin learning more about wild animals. Visits to zoos with Southern Californian wildlife on display can also be worthwhile educational experiences. And there's no substitute for firsthand field study. You've found tracks, now you know what animals to look for. Read my notes on diet, put some bait out, sit quietly downwind with binoculars for a few hours, and see what comes along. Or follow the tracks a while. Use your imagination and common sense, and you'll be amazed at how much you can learn, and how rewarding the experiences can be.

As you use this book, remember that track identification is an inexact science. The illustrations in this book represent average *adult* tracks on *ideal* surfaces. But many of the tracks you encounter in the wild will be those of smaller-than-average animals, particularly in late spring and early summer. There are also larger-than-average animals, and injured or deformed ones, and animals that act unpredictably. Some creatures walk sideways on occasion. Most vary their gait so that in a single set of tracks front prints may fall ahead of, behind, or beneath the rear. In addition, ground conditions are usually less than ideal in the wild, and animals often dislodge debris, which may further confuse the picture. Use this book as a guide, but anticipate a lot of variations.

In attempting to identify tracks, remember that their size can vary greatly depending on the type of ground surface—sand that is loose or firm, wet or dry; a thin layer of mud over hard earth; deep soft mud; various lightly frozen surfaces; firm or loose dirt; dry or moist snow; a dusting of snow or frost over various surfaces; and so on. Note the surface from which the illustrations are taken and interpret what you find in nature accordingly.

You should also be aware that droplets from trees, windblown debris, and the like often leave a variety of marks on the ground that could be mistaken for animal tracks. While studying tracks, look around for and be aware of nonanimal factors that might have left "tracks" of their own.

The range notes pertain only to Southern California. Many track makers in this book also live elsewhere in North America. Range and habitat remarks are general guidelines because both are subject to change, from variations in both animal and human populations, climatic factors, pollution levels, acts of God, and so forth.

The size, height, and weight listed for each animal are those for average adults. Size refers to length from nose to tip of tail; height, the distance from ground to shoulder.

A few well-known species have been left out of this book: moles and bats, for example, which generally leave no above-ground tracks. Animals that may be common elsewhere but are rare, or occur only in the margins of Southern California, have also been omitted. Some species herein, particularly small rodents and birds, stand as representatives of groups of related species. In such cases the featured species is the one most commonly encountered and widely distributed. Related species, often with similar tracks, are listed in the notes. Where their tracks can be distinguished, guidelines for doing so are provided.

If you encounter an injured animal or an apparently orphaned infant, you may be tempted to take it home and care for it. Do not do so. Instead, report the animal to local authorities, who are better able to care for it. In addition, federal and state laws often strictly control the handling of wild animals. This is always the case with species classified as *rare* or *endangered*. Removing animals from the wild may be illegal.

TRACKING TIPS

At times you'll be lucky enough to find a perfectly clear and precise track that gives you all the information you need to identify the maker with a quick glance through this book. More often the track will be imperfect or fragmented. Following the tracks may lead you to a more readily identifiable print. Or maybe you have the time and inclination to follow an animal whose identity you already know in order to learn more about its habits, characteristics, and behavior.

Here are some tips for improving your tracking skills:

1. If you don't see tracks, look for disturbances—leaves or twigs in unnatural positions, debris or stones that appear to have been moved or turned. Stones become bleached on top over time, so a stone with its darker side up or sideways has recently been dislodged.

2. Push small sticks into the ground to mark individual signs. These will help you keep your bearings and "map out" the animal's general direction of travel.

3. Check immovable objects like trees, logs, and boulders along the route of travel for scratches, scuff marks, or fragments of hair.

4. Look at the ground from different angles, from standing height, from kneeling height, and if possible, from an elevated position in a tree or on a boulder or rise.

5. On very firm surfaces, place your cheek on the ground and observe the surface, first through one eye, then the other, looking for unnatural depressions or disturbances.

6. Study the trail from as many different directions as possible. Trail signs may become obvious as the angle of light between them and your eyes changes, especially if dew, dust, or rain covers some parts of the ground surface.

7. Check for tracks beneath recently disturbed leaves or fallen debris.

8. Try not to focus you attention so narrowly that you lose sight of the larger patterns of the country around you.

9. Keep your bearings. Some animals circle back if they become aware of being followed. If you find yourself following signs in a circular path, try waiting motionless and silent for a while, observing behind you.

10. Look ahead as far as possible as you follow signs. Animals take the paths of least resistance, so look for trails or runways. You may even catch sight of your quarry.

11. Animals are habitual in their movements between burrows, den sites, sources of water and food, temporary shelters, prominent trees, and so on. As you track and look ahead, try to anticipate where the creature might be going.

12. Stalk as you track; move as carefully and quietly as possible.

The secrets to successful tracking are patience and knowledge. Whenever you see an animal leaving tracks, go look at them and note the activity you observed. When you find and identify tracks, make little sketches alongside the book's illustrations, showing cluster patterns, or individual impressions that are different from those drawn. Make notes about what you learn in the wilds and from other readings. Eventually, you will build a body of knowledge from your own experience, and your future attempts at track identification will become easier and more certain.

This book is largely a compilation of the author's personal experiences. You experiences with certain animals and their tracks may be identical, similar, or quite different. If you notice a discrepancy or find tracks that are not included in this book, carefully note your observations, or even amend the illustrations or text to reflect your own experiences.

Mammals
Reptiles
Amphibians
Invertebrates

INVERTEBRATES

The smallest track impressions you are likely to encounter in nature will probably look something like those illustrated at the right.

From left to right, the illustration shows tracks of two common beetles, a centipede, and a cricket. The track of an earthworm crosses from the lower left to upper right corner.

You might initially mistake a variety of scuffs and scratches left by windblown or otherwise dislodged debris, the imprint of raindrops that have fallen from overhanging limbs, impressions left by the smallest mice, or even the perplexing calligraphy of toads for insect marks. If you have more than a square foot or so of ground surface to scrutinize, however, you will usually find that insect tracks form a recognizably connected line; the extremely shallow depth of the trail of imprints is also a good clue that a very lightweight being has passed by.

With literally millions of species out there, trying to identify the insect that made a particular track can be challenging, but there are times when you can follow a trail and find, at the end, either the bug itself, or a burrow that could yield its resident with a little patient and careful excavation on your part. If you spend enough time in one area, you will begin to observe specific species in the act of making their tracks, and that goes a long way toward track recognition—for any size of animal.

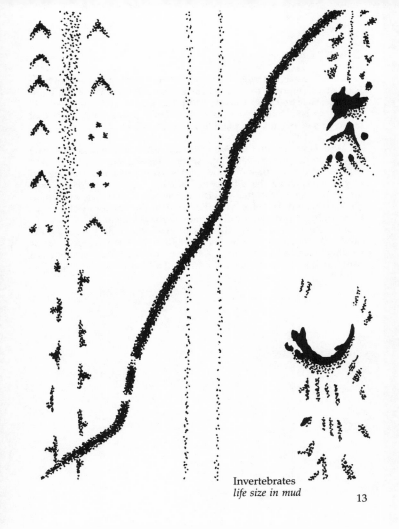

Invertebrates
life size in mud

13

GHOST CRAB

Ocypode albicans

Class: Crustacea. **Order:** Decapoda. **Range and habitat:** throughout Southern California; on sandy beaches, usually just above the high-tide line. **Size and weight:** body width less than 2 inches, legspan less than 4 inches; fraction of an ounce. **Diet:** aquatic and terrestrial micro-organisms, insects, plankton. **Sounds:** silent.

Ghost crabs are the entertaining and extremely quick little pale gray- to buff-colored crabs that seem to spend most of their lives tossing sand from their burrows and scurrying around foraging for tiny morsels along the tidelines of beaches, particularly in the evening. They run so fast that you can barely focus your eyes on them in the light of midday; when you glimpse their fleeting forms at dusk or by moonlight, you might truly think you're seeing ghosts.

But if their speed makes them nearly invisible, their tracks and excavations, common and easily recognized on the sandy, warm-weather beaches of Southern California and elsewhere around the world, remain to be studied at leisure and to reveal their secrets.

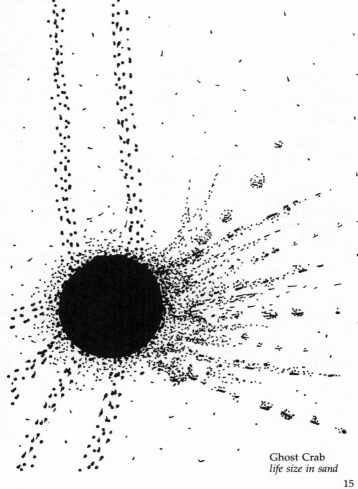

Ghost Crab
life size in sand

15

LITTLE POCKET MOUSE   *Perognathus longimembris*

Order: Rodentia (gnawing mammals). **Family:** Cricetidae (New World rats and mice). **Range and habitat:** throughout most of Southern California; variable, usually in valleys and on hillsides, in sagebrush, creosote brush, and sandy cactus country. **Size and weight:** 5 inches; less than ½ ounce. **Diet:** primarily seeds; occasionally fruit, berries, insects. **Sounds:** generally silent.

The little pocket mouse, one of the smallest Southern California mammals, certainly leaves the smallest recognizable clusters of mammalian tracks. This tiny, light brown, pointy-nosed, white-bellied mouse leads a very subdued, low-profile existence, ranging only a couple hundred yards from its burrow, an inconspicuous hole in the ground slightly less than an inch in diameter, often with a small mound of fine soil near the entrance. The pocket mouse may live for up to seven years in its little territory, raising one or two litters of offspring each year, which are, or course, important items in the diets of a great number of predators.

The little pocket mouse is the most widespread Southern California pocket mouse species, but similar tracks could also have been left by any of seven other barely distinguishable locally common species. You will, at any rate, be able to recognize pocket mouse tracks by the small size and extremely narrow overall cluster width, with leaps of no more than 4½ inches. Although pocket mouse tracks might be confused with those of a small kangaroo rat if they are not too clear, pocket mice generally use single burrows, while kangaroo rats tend to use multiple burrows and mounds, with well-worn trails connecting them.

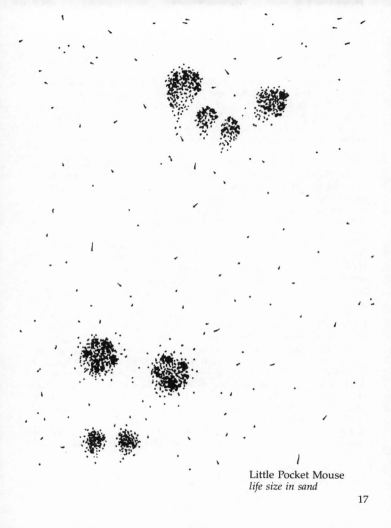

Little Pocket Mouse
life size in sand

17

CACTUS MOUSE
Peromyscus eremicus

Order: Rodentia (gnawing mammals). **Family:** Cricetidae (New World rats and mice). **Range and habitat:** common throughout Southern California; in deserts, rocks, cactus and yucca stands. **Size and weight:** 11 inches; 1 ounce. **Diet:** omnivorous, primarily seeds but also mushrooms and other fungi, berries, herbs, insects, larvae, and carrion. **Sounds:** occasional faint chirps, squeaks, and chattering.

The cactus mouse is a medium-sized, long-tailed mouse with white underside and feet, pointy nose, and fairly large ears. Well-adapted for life in the desert, the cactus mouse tolerates higher air temperatures and needs less water than most other mice. It makes up the main diet of many carnivorous birds and mammals, but is not so completely defenseless as you might think—it may bite if handled carelessly.

The cactus mouse usually leaves a distinctive track pattern: four-print clusters about 1½ inches wide, walking or leaping up to 9 inches, with the tail dragging occasionally. As with any creature so small, its tracks are distinct only on rare occasions when surface conditions are perfect. More often you find merely clusters of tiny dimples in the mud or snow.

Such tracks could also be made by other "white-footed mice" (e.g., house, deer, California, canyon, brush, or piñon mice) or even by other, more distantly related mice (e.g., western harvest, pocket and grasshopper mice, or various meadow mice and voles). Give or take an inch and a few fractions of an ounce, they're all quite similar in appearance. You will need a good pictorial field guide and some patient field work to make positive identifications. Mouse tracks can, however, be distinguished from those of the shrew, whose feet are about the same size: mouse track clusters are wider than those of shrews, and shrews tend to scuttle along or burrow under snow, rather than run and leap. Also, if you follow mouse tracks, more often than not you will find evidence of seed eating; shrews are strictly carnivorous.

Cactus Mouse
life size in mud

ORNATE SHREW   *Sorex ornatus*

Order: Insectivora (insect-eating mammals, including shrews, moles, and bats). **Family:** Soricidae (shrews). **Range and habitat:** coastal and central Southern California; very adaptable; along streams, in brushy areas, valleys, foothills, and yellow pine forests. **Size and weight:** 5 inches; 1 ounce. **Diet:** slugs, snails, spiders, insects, and larvae; occasionally mice and carrion. **Sounds:** commonly silent.

The ornate shrew is a vole-shaped creature with shorter legs, a slightly more elongated body, and a long, pointed snout. Shrew dentists have a big advantage in distinguishing the various species, because variations in unicuspid teeth are all that differentiate many of them. *All* shrews are little eating machines, though, with extremely high metabolisms, evidenced by heartbeat and respiration rates around 1200 per minute. In fact, shrews consume more than their own body weight in food on a daily basis.

Shrews' constant and aggressive quest for food makes their tracks, in general, fairly easy to identify. The animals move around with more single-minded purpose than mice or voles, usually in series of short hops in which the rear feet fall over the tracks of the front feet; the tails often drag, leaving the distinctive pattern shown, usually less than an inch in width. When individual impressions are more distinct, you may notice that shrews have five toes on both fore- and hind feet (most micelike creatures have four toes on the forefeet).

Similar tracks in the arid southeastern portions of Southern California were probably made by the desert shrew, whose range overlaps that of the ornate shrew.

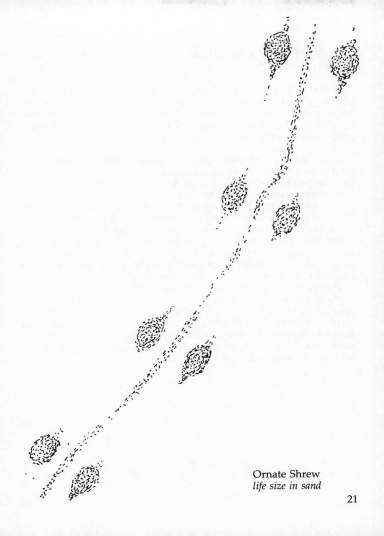

Ornate Shrew
life size in sand

BOTTA'S POCKET GOPHER
Valley pocket gopher

Thomomys bottae

Order: Rodentia (gnawing mammals). **Family:** Geomyidae (pocket gophers). **Range and habitat:** throughout Southern California; in deserts, fields, pastures, grasslands, and on roadsides. **Size and weight:** 9 inches; 6 ounces. **Diet:** various foliage, twigs, bark, roots and tubers. **Sounds:** silent.

Botta's pocket gopher is a peculiar, highly evolved burrowing rodent named for the fur-lined cheek pockets in which it carries both food and nesting materials; the pockets can be turned inside out to empty their contents and for cleaning.

It looks like a small buff to grayish rat except that its large, yellowish front teeth are always showing; its lips close behind the teeth, so the animal can gnaw through earth and roots during tunneling without getting dirt in its mouth. Pocket gophers spend most of their lives in extensive tunnel systems. Signs of pocket gopher activity include tracks or tooth marks on limbs near their tunnel entrances, and plugged earthen mounds near those entrances.

The tracks are similar in size to those of a chipmunk, but the pocket gopher's elongated heel pads leave larger impressions. The most distinctive characteristic of pocket gopher tracks, however, is the imprint of the five toes on both front and rear feet; the relatively long digging claws on its front feet leave prominent marks, and the distance between the toe and the claw marks is greater than with any other similar-sized creature.

Botta's Pocket Gopher
life size in mud

23

WESTERN TOAD   *Bufo boreas*

Order: Salientia (frogs, toads, and allies). **Family:** Bufonidae (true toads). **Range and habitat:** widespread throughout Southern California, except the arid southeastern portions; in moist woodlands and adjoining areas, wherever insects are abundant, usually but not necessarily within a mile of permanent dampness. **Size and weight:** 4 inches; 2 ounces. **Diet:** insects. **Sounds:** high-pitched musical trills.

Toads are small, froglike animals with dry, warty skin, in a variety of reddish, brown, and gray colors. They are primarily nocturnal, but can be seen at dawn or dusk, or even by day, crouching in a little niche, waiting for bugs. Unlike frogs, toads often travel fairly far from sources of water. In fact, red-spotted toads, which inhabit much of the arid region of southeastern California, receive moisture only through diet for most of the year. All toads do require water for breeding, however; look for their long, ropy strings of eggs in stagnant pond water.

Individual toad tracks can be confusing and might be mistaken for the tiny dimples and scratchings of tracks left by small mice or insects. A toad tends to sit quietly waiting for insects to fly past it, at which time it takes a few leaps in the direction of wing noise, snares the bug with its long, sticky tongue, then repeats the procedure. Thus it may change direction over earlier prints, which makes a very confusing picture on the ground.

Toad tracks generally consist of nothing more distinct than a trail of little holes and scrapes, with impressions that sometimes resemble little toad hands. The distinguishing characteristics are the mode of wandering, the short rows of four or five round dimples left by the toes of the larger rear feet, and the drag marks often left by the feet as the toad moves forward; those toe-drag marks point in the direction of travel.

You won't get warts from handling toads, but make sure you don't have insect repellent or other caustic substances on your hands that might injure the toad's sensitive skin.

Western Toad
life size in mud

25

COUCH'S SPADEFOOT TOAD   *Scaphiopus couchi*
WESTERN SPADEFOOT TOAD   *Scaphiopus hammondi*

Order: Salientia (frogs, toads, and allies). **Family:** Pelobatidae.
Range and habitat: southeastern corner of Southern California; in dry
terrain, shortgrass prairie, mesquite savannah, and creosote bush
desert. **Size and weight:** 3 inches; 1 ounce. **Diet:** insects. **Sounds:** a
bleat, like that of a lamb, lasting one second; very noisy chorus, au-
dible from a great distance.

Unique among leaping amphibians, spadefoot toads have wedge-
or sickle-shaped bony "spades" on the inner surfaces of each hind
foot, which they use to burrow into the ground. Two species of
spadefoot toads live in Southern California; both are variably col-
ored, with light stripes and black marbling above, and mostly white
bellies. The larger Couch's spadefoot (*S. couchi*), up to 3½ inches in
length, is found in shortgrass prairies, mesquite savannahs, and creosote brush desert areas; the western spadefoot (*S. hammondi*), measuring less than 2½ inches, lives in a variety of arid and semiarid
western parts of Southern California, wherever soils are favorable for
digging. Both of these spadefoots exhibit unique adaptations for
their arid habitats: they burrow into the ground or modify existing
burrows of small mammals, remaining underground by day throughout dry periods; and they have greatly accelerated reproductive cycles
keyed to rainy periods, with tadpoles transforming into adults in two
to six weeks.

The spadefoots are gregarious; a chorus of their songs—bleats or
trills lasting about a second—will help you locate these nocturnal
creatures by night. By day, look closely and walk carefully. The semi-
circular impressions left by their digging spades readily distinguish
spadefoot tracks from those of other small creatures, and you will
most likely find the toads in their burrows very near by.

Couch's Spadefoot Toad 27
life size in sand

WHITE-TAILED ANTELOPE SQUIRREL
Ammospermophilus leucurus

Order: Rodentia (gnawing mammals). **Family:** Sciuridae (squirrels). **Range and habitat:** most of central and eastern Southern California; from low sagebrush deserts and rocky areas with scattered trees to gravelly foothills. **Size and weight:** 9 inches; 2 ounces. **Diet:** vegetation, berries, grains, seeds, insects, and carrion. **Sounds:** shrill and persistent "chip, chip."

The most widespread ground-living squirrel species in Southern California, the white-tailed antelope squirrel is difficult to distinguish from locally common Harris's antelope squirrel, the Panamint, lodgepole, and Merriam's chipmunks, and the round-tailed and golden-mantled ground squirrels. Most have more or less distinctive black and white stripes from nose to moderately bushy tail; they hold their tails over their backs as they leap and scurry over the ground.

The track patterns of all these small squirrels are roughly 2 inches in width, with 7 to 15 inches between clusters of prints. They usually run up on their toes, so rear-heel imprints may not show at all or may be less clear. The hind-foot tracks (five-toed) almost always fall closer together than and in front of the forefoot tracks (four-toed), typical of the tracks of all squirrel family members.

White-tailed Antelope Squirrel
life size in mud

DESERT WOODRAT   *Neotoma lepida*

Order: Rodentia (gnawing mammals). **Family:** Cricetidae (New World rats and mice). **Range and habitat:** widespread throughout all of Southern California; in desert and piñon-juniper areas. **Size and weight:** 15 inches; 1¼ pounds. **Diet:** spiny cacti, yucca pods, nuts, seeds, berries, green vegetation. **Sounds:** occasionally rattles tail against dry vegetation.

This native American rat is active year round but it is seldom sighted in the wild, as it is generally nocturnal. The desert woodrat is slightly larger than imported Norway and black rats, and has a furry, not scaly, tail. Woodrats avoid human habitations, although they may "borrow" shiny objects from campsites.

Three species are present in California. The dusky-footed woodrat is the slightly larger model of brushlands and coastal forests; the white-throated woodrat overlaps the desert woodrat's range in the arid southeastern portion of the region. All are pale grayish brown and ratlike in appearance.

The desert woodrat is a skilled and frequent climber of cacti, and it usually uses old ground squirrel or kangaroo rat burrows.

Woodrats have fairly stubby toes, four on the forefeet and five on the hind, that usually leave uniquely shaped tracks with no claw marks. The tracks are roughly in line when walking and grouped as illustrated when running, with 8 or more inches separating the clusters of prints. Like most small rodents, when woodrats leap, their front feet land first, followed by the back feet, which come down ahead of the front imprints, providing the spring into the next leap. If the characteristic stubby-toed imprints are not clear, the short spacing relative to foot size should help distinguish woodrat tracks from similar ones made by other animals of comparable size.

Desert Woodrat
life size in mud

LONG-TAILED WEASEL   *Mustela frenata*

Order: Carnivora (flesh-eating mammals). **Family:** Mustelidae (the weasel family). **Range and habitat:** absent only from the arid eastern portion of Southern California; most habitats where water is nearby. **Size and weight:** variable, generally averages 12-14 inches; 6-10 ounces. **Diet:** small rodents, chipmunks, birds, amphibians. **Sounds:** may shriek or squeal when alarmed or making a kill; also purrs, chatters, hisses.

The long-tailed weasel is an adaptable, inquisitive, and aggressive little carnivore with a thin, elongated body and tail. Active day and night, it will climb and swim but generally confines its activities to an agile pursuit of prey on the ground, where it also finds various burrows. In portions of this region that have cold winters, its summer coat (brown, with white belly and black tail tip) often molts to white with black tail tip, or a mottled condition of partial molt.

The long-tailed weasel varies its gait frequently, alternating leaps with a variety of other modes of travel. Its stride is usually from 12 to 20 inches, with leaps of up to 50 inches. If close study doesn't reveal fifth-toe prints, which is often the case with tracks of weasel family members, individual weasel tracks can be tough to distinguish from those of many squirrels or rabbits. But weasels characteristically alternate long and short bounds, or leave lines of doubled-over tracks with occasional tail drag marks, whereas rabbits and squirrels tend to leave four separate prints in each cluster without tail drags. The latter often leave evidence of vegetarian diets, whereas weasels are strictly carnivorous.

Long-tailed Weasel
life size in mud

33

MERRIAM'S KANGAROO RAT   *Dipodomys merriami*

Order: Rodentia (gnawing mammals). **Family:** Heteromyidae (kangaroo mice and rats). **Range and habitat:** most east and central parts of Southern California; on dry, grassy plains and open, brushy foothills, preferring gravelly ground. **Size and weight:** 9 inches, most of which is tail; 2½ ounces. **Diet:** seeds and great variety of vegetation. **Sounds:** thumps feet when alarmed.

At least eight kangaroo rat species can be found in various parts of Southern California. Merriam's is widespread, and its characteristics are representative of the lot: a chubby rat with buff or gray fur, white belly and feet, white stripes across the outer thigh meeting at the base of the tail, strong hind legs with oversized rear feet, and a very long, bushy-tipped tail. It is nocturnal, prefers arid or semiarid habitats, and lives in extensive burrow systems, which are often—especially in sandy areas—as much as 3 feet high and 12 feet or so in diameter, with many entrance holes. Around these burrows, and along the paths connecting them to feeding places or other mounds, you often find cut plant fragments. Kangaroo rats rarely travel more than about 50 feet from these not inconspicuous nests.

There is great size variation among Southern California's kangaroo rats, ranging from Merriam's, the smallest (about 9 inches long), to the desert kangaroo rat, whose tail alone may be longer than that. Some species have four toes on their hind feet, some have five. All have the same basic track pattern. When a kangaroo rat moves slowly, as while feeding, most of its 1½- to 2-inch hind prints are visible, as are impressions of the smaller forepaws and the long tail. At speed, however, when the animal is making leaps of 3 to 9 feet, only the rear toes contact the ground. Combined with other signs, the resulting widely spaced pairs of prints clearly indicate the passage of these interesting rodents. Similar, but smaller, more closely spaced tracks are made by pocket and kangaroo mice.

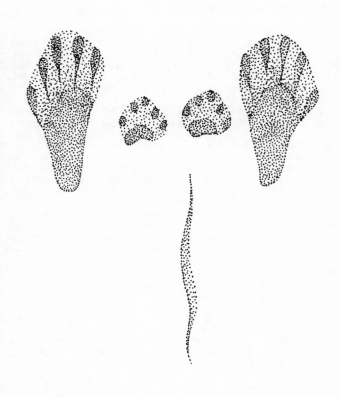

Merriam's Kangaroo Rat
life size in sand

CALIFORNIA GROUND SQUIRREL   *Spermophilus beecheyi*

Order: Rodentia (gnawing mammals). **Family:** Sciuridae (squirrels). **Range and habitat:** absent only from the arid southeast corner of Southern California; in nearly all open areas, avoids thick chaparral and dense forest. **Size and weight:** 17 inches; 1½ pounds. **Diet:** omnivorous, including green vegetation, seeds, acorns, mushrooms, fruit, berries, birds, eggs, insects. **Sounds:** loud chirp when alarmed.

Common, widespread and active by day, the California ground squirrel is easy to sight and recognize. The largest ground squirrel in the state, it looks like a very fat western gray squirrel with an only slightly fluffy tail. Its coat is pale brownish gray, with lightly speckled back and rump. Its gray tail is fringed in white, and across the top of its shoulders, there is a V of darker fur that points forward. The California ground squirrel lives in a complex of burrows sometimes 200 feet or more in length, and rarely ventures far from the interconnected system of runways between its entrance mounds.

Although the squirrel may climb into a bush to bask in the early morning sun, it normally stays on the ground. It lives in loose colonies, with four or five adults sharing an acre or so of space. Throughout most of Southern California, the California ground squirrel spends the hot months of summer and early fall asleep in its nest below ground. At higher elevations, it may reverse the pattern.

Regrettably, the California ground squirrel does significant damage to crops and pastureland, and its fleas often carry plague.

California ground squirrel tracks are easy to identify. For one thing, no other large squirrel shares the open, grassy habitat of this species. The track pattern is characteristic of the squirrel family, usually a cluster of four prints less than 3 inches wide, with the front footprints closer together and slightly behind those left by the rear feet. These ground squirrels have five toes on both front and rear feet, but the front thumbs are so truncated that they do not leave marks. Front toe imprints tend to be slightly lopsided or offset toward the outside of the line of travel. Walking stride is about 2 inches, with leaps of 10 to 18 inches.

California Ground Squirrel
life size in mud

37

NORTHERN FLYING SQUIRREL   *Glaucomys sabrinus*

Order: Rodentia (gnawing mammals). **Family:** Sciuridae (squirrels). **Range and habitat:** portions of Angeles, San Bernardino, and Cleveland national forests; in coniferous and, occasionally, mixed forests at higher altitudes. **Size and weight:** 11 inches; 6 ounces. **Diet:** bark, fungi, lichen, seeds, insects, eggs, and carrion. **Sounds:** generally silent; occasionally makes chirpy, birdlike noises.

Northern flying squirrels are nocturnal, so chances are that you will only see their tracks, unless you happen to knock against or cut down one of the hollow trees in which they are fond of nesting; in that case, if a small gray squirrel runs out, you've had a rare glimpse of the northern flying squirrel.

In warm areas, the northern flying squirrel doesn't leave much evidence of its passage. It lives mostly in trees, using the fur-covered membrane that extends along each side of its body from the front to the rear legs to glide between trees and occasionally from tree to earth, where it usually leaves no marks on the ground cover of its forest habitat. If snow has fallen, however, you may find its tracks leading away from what looks like a miniature, scuffed snow-angel, the pattern left when the squirrel lands at the end of an aerial descent. The tracks may wander around a bit if the squirrel has foraged for morsels, but they will lead back to the trunk of a nearby tree before long.

Northern Flying Squirrel
life size in sand

LIZARDS
Order: Squamata

Lizards are the largest group of living reptiles worldwide, with 115 species in North America alone. In Southern California, about twenty-five lizard species exist in a bewildering array of sizes, colors, and shapes, from tiny geckos less than 3 inches long, to Gila monsters measuring up to 2 feet from nose to tip of tail.

Although pinning down which species made a particular track may prove difficult or impossible, you should find it fairly easy to recognize that the trail was left by a lizard of some sort. Portions of the low-slung belly and/or tail usually drag along the surface it's walking on, and the five-toed feet alternate, rather than fall side by side, distinguishing the tracks from those left by small mammals. At times, the waving tail may brush away some details of the footprints. Turtles sometimes leave similar trails, but a turtle with the same size feet as a lizard would usually leave a wider trail.

The straddle and gait of lizards vary widely depending on their size, of course; the illustration represents a lizard of about 8 inches, nose to tail tip.

Lizard
life size in sand

SNAKES
Order: Squamata

There are 115 species of snakes living in North America, 19 of which are poisonous. They vary in length from 6 inches to nearly 9 feet. Many species of snakes in a variety of sizes and colors live in various habitats of Southern California, including most of the poisonous snakes of North America: the large, aggressive and quite poisonous western diamondback rattlesnake as well as ten other rattlesnake species, including the sidewinder. When hiking the wild country, watch where you step and look carefully for snakes as well as their tracks!

Snake tracks are easy to recognize, and the width of the snake is pretty easy to guess. It's usually difficult to tell a snake's direction of travel from its trail over flat ground, because snakes don't usually move fast enough to dislodge peripheral debris. If you can follow the trail far enough, however, you may find a place where the elevation or type of ground surface changes; there, with careful investigation, you might find some minute clues about the direction of travel.

It is likewise difficult to identify a snake by tracks, except for the sidewinder, which leaves a trail of parallel J-shaped marks behind it as it flips its body repeatedly along the ground of its arid, sandy habitat.

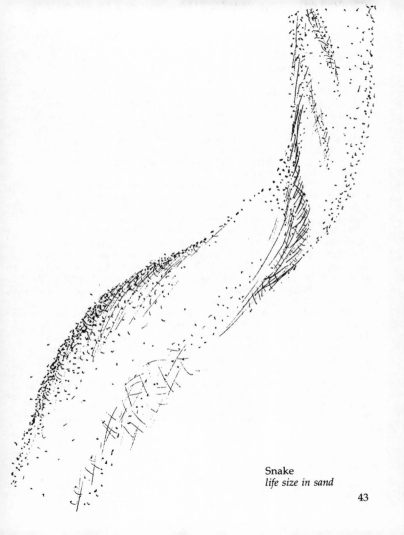

Snake
life size in sand

LAND TURTLES
Order: Testudines

Forty-eight species of turtles live in North America. Their tracks are fairly common near bodies of water, and, less frequently, in moist woodlands. These peculiar creatures predate dinosaurs and have a body structure unlike any other animal: a shell composed of expanded ribs, limbs extending from within the turtle's rib cage, and a horny beak instead of teeth. The shell is divided into two parts: the upper, called the carapace, and the lower, which is hinged in some species, called the plastron.

The track left by the turtle is determined by the shape of the plastron and how high the turtle is holding its shell from the ground surface, which in turn depends on the species of turtle, the length of its legs, and the firmness of the surface it's walking over.

The track drawn on the left (the turtle moved toward the top of the page) shows that the turtle dragged most of its plastron, leaving a trail that obscured a lot of the indistinct prints left by its appendages; the drag trail looks similar to that of a tail-dragging beaver, but a shell-dragging turtle trail goes straight for several feet or more, until the turtle changes direction, whereas a beaver's tail-dragging trail zigzags slightly over 6 or 8 inches.

The second turtle trail, drawn on the right, was made on a firmer surface by a turtle that held its plastron off the surface; only the turtle's tail dragged, leaving a narrow, almost straight line. Individual footprints were merely smudges in some places, where the reptile had slipped, but where the turtle took firm steps, the tracks showed its feet and strong claws.

There are only two species of land turtles within Southern California: the western pond turtle, 3 to 7 inches, of wet habitats; and the desert tortoise, 9 to 14 inches, of arid regions. Tracks can be identified, thus, by the humidity of the habitat in which they are located.

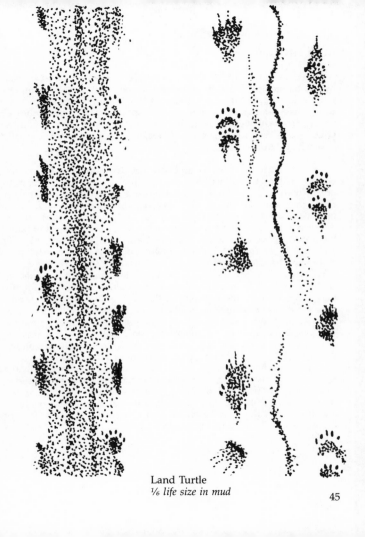

Land Turtle
⅙ life size in mud

45

BULLFROG   *Rana catesbiana*

Order: Salientia (frogs, toads, and allies). **Family:** Ranidae (true frogs). **Range and habitat:** widespread throughout most of Southern California except from Twentynine Palms Marine Corps Base eastward; in ponds, lakes, marshes and swamps, year-round bodies of water. **Size and weight:** body 5-8 inches, with long legs; 4 ounces. **Diet:** insects. **Sounds:** low-pitched croaks, deep jug-o-rum, especially at dawn and dusk.

Of the eighty-one species of frogs that live north of Mexico, the bullfrog is the largest. Varying in color from a mottled dark gray to green, with an off-white belly, bullfrogs live in or very near water because they must keep their skin wet and they breed in water. They use distinctive vocalizations to signal each other and to attract mates. the 4- to 6-inch long vegetarian tadpoles take up to two years to transform into carnivorous adults. As with all toads and frogs, be sure your hands are free from insect repellent or other caustic substances before you handle a bullfrog as it has particularly sensitive skin.

Frogs walk or hop in a more plantigrade manner than toads, so their tracks tend to be more easily recognizable. You will commonly find impressions of the full soles of their feet and might even be able to see that their hind feet are webbed, except the last joint of the longest toe, although these delicate membranes don't always imprint. The toed-in imprints of the small front feet combined with a straddle of 5 or 6 inches should leave no doubt about the identity of bullfrog tracks, even if the hind-foot impressions are less than distinct.

Only two other true frogs live in California, both primarily in the western half of the state. The tracks of the red-legged frog and yellow-legged frog are nearly identical to those of the bullfrog in shape, but considerably smaller in foot size, width of straddle, length of stride and leaps, and depth of impression in soft surfaces. Adult frogs of these species average 2 to 3 inches in length.

Bullfrog
life size in mud

WESTERN SPOTTED SKUNK
Civet cat, hydrophobia cat

Spilogale gracilis

Order: Carnivora (flesh-eating mammals). **Family:** Mustelidae (the weasel family). **Range and habitat:** widespread throughout Southern California; in brushy or sparsely wooded areas along streams, among boulders, and in prairies. **Size and weight:** 25 inches; 3 pounds. **Diet:** omnivorous, including rats, mice, birds, insects, eggs, carrion, seeds, fruit, and occasionally vegetation. **Sounds:** usually silent.

The spotted skunk is the smallest and most visually interesting of the North American skunks. About the size of a small house cat, with an assortment of white spots and streaks over its black coat, the spotted skunk has finer, silkier fur than other skunks, is quicker and more agile, and occasionally climbs trees, although it doesn't stay aloft for long. It is primarily nocturnal, but you might see it at dawn or dusk, or foraging during the daylight in winter, when hunger keeps it active. Skunks have the most highly effective scent glands of all the mustelids and can, when severely provoked, shoot a fine spray of extremely irritating methyl mercaptan as far as 25 feet. Everyone knows what that smells like.

Skunk tracks are all similar, with five toes on each foot leaving prints, toenail prints commonly visible, and front tracks slightly less flat-footed than rear. Only size and irregular stride may help distinguish the tracks of the spotted skunk from those of the twice-as-large striped skunk. Spotted skunk tracks will be about 1¼ inches long at most; adult striped skunks leave tracks up to 2 inches in length. On the other hand, the quick spotted skunk leaves a foot or more between *clusters* of prints when running, while the larger striped skunk lopes along with only about 5 or 6 inches between more strung-out track groups.

Because skunks can hold most land animals at bay with their formidable scent, owls are their chief predators. If you are following a skunk trail that ends suddenly, with perhaps a bit of black and white fur remaining mysteriously where the tracks disappear, you might be able to guess what transpired.

Western Spotted Skunk
life size in mud

RINGTAIL   *Bassariscus astutus*
Ringtail cat, miner's cat, civet cat, cacomistle

Order: Carnivora (flesh-eating mammals). **Family:** Bassariscidae (ringtails). **Range and habitat:** throughout most of Southern California; most common in chaparral, rocky ridges, caves and cliffs, talus slopes, occasionally in forested areas. **Size and weight:** 30 inches, half of which is tail; 2 pounds. **Diet:** small animals, bats, birds, insects, fruit. **Sounds:** a coughing bark or whimper when alarmed.

The secretive, seldom seen ringtail has large round ears, white eye rings, an elongated gray body, and a distinctive bushy black-and-white-striped tail that is fully as long as its body. This strictly nocturnal animal tends to lead a solitary, inconspicuous life in relatively isolated terrain.

Ringtail tracks are uncommon and, when found, not easy to distinguish from those of the spotted skunk. But because ringtails have semiretractile claws, their tracks are often quite catlike, whereas those of spotted skunks usually show claw marks. Ringtail pad imprints also tend to be less elongated than those of spotted skunks, ringtails are more likely to leave tail brush marks than spotted skunks, and ringtails usually leave doubled-over track pairs 6 to 10 inches apart, while spotted skunks leave very irregular trails of single prints, or clusters of four tracks.

Ringtail
life size in mud

STRIPED SKUNK   *Mephitis mephitis*

Order: Carnivora (flesh-eating mammals). **Family:** Mustelidae (weasels and skunks). **Range and habitat:** throughout Southern California, absent only from extremely arid areas; in semiopen country, mixed woods, brushland, and open fields. **Size and weight:** 24 inches, 10 pounds. **Diet:** omnivorous, including mice, eggs, insects, grubs, fruit, carrion. **Sounds:** usually silent.

Often found dead along highways, this cat-sized skunk is easily recognized by the two broad stripes running the length of its back, meeting at head and shoulders to form a cap. A thin white stripe runs down its face. Active year round, it is chiefly nocturnal but may be sighted shortly after sunset or at dawn, snuffling around for food. It seeks shelter beneath buildings as well as in ground burrows or other protected den sites, and protects itself, when threatened, with a fine spray of extremely irritating methyl mercaptan.

Striped skunk tracks are similar to but larger than those of the smaller spotted skunk, and its elongated heel pads are often apparent because it's not as quick, agile, or high-strung as its smaller cousin. With five closely spaced toes and claws on all feet usually leaving marks, its tracks can't be mistaken for any others of its size; the spacing is distinctive too: generally less than 6 inches between track groups, whether they consist of walking pairs or strung-out loping groups of four tracks.

Striped Skunk
life size in mud

WESTERN GRAY SQUIRREL   *Sciurus griseus*

Order: Rodentia (gnawing mammals). **Family:** Sciuridae (squirrels). **Range and habitat:** throughout most of Southern California except extremely arid regions; in hardwood (especially oak), pine, or mixed hardwood-evergreen forests and parklands, occasionally nearby in swamp fringes. **Size and weight:** 20 inches, 1½ pounds. **Diet:** mostly acorn and pine seeds, also various nuts, seeds, fungi, insects and larvae, some vegetation. **Sounds:** variety of rapid, raspy barks.

This large, light-gray squirrel with its long, upraised bushy tail is such a common park animal that most Californians are familiar with it. Active all day, year round, the western gray squirrel nests in tree cavities, or in conspicuous nests made of sticks and shredded bark, usually 20 feet or more above the ground. It spends a lot of time on the ground searching for nuts and seeds, ranging widely from its home trees.

Because of its wandering habits, the western gray squirrel leaves a lot of tracks in areas traveled through by other similar-sized animals. Consequently, partial track impressions can be confusing. Most of the time, the gray squirrel scampers rather than walks, so its long rear heels don't leave prints. The real keys to recognizing the tracks of a western gray squirrel are the number of toes—four on the front feet, five on the rear—and knowing the general track characteristics common to all members of the squirrel family. First, impressions of the entire toes, rather than just the tips, are often present. Second, two middle toes of the front feet and the three middle toes of the rear feet are nearly always out ahead of, and parallel to, the heel pads, with the outer toes splayed out to the sides. Track sets are normally about 4½ inches wide and spaced 2 to 3 feet apart.

Western Gray Squirrel
life size in sand

KIT FOX   *Vulpes macrotis*
Swift fox, Channel Island fox

   Order: Carnivora (flesh-eating mammals). **Family:** Canidae
(wolves, coyotes, and foxes). **Range and habitat:** south and east from
Bakersfield to the Mexican border, and on all Channel Islands except
Anacapa and Santa Barbara; adaptable, but prefers open, level, sandy
ground. **Size and weight:** 30 inches; 5 pounds. **Diet:** omnivorous, opportunistic feeders; mainly insects, berries, fruit, birds, eggs, mice,
and carrion. **Sounds:** yaps, whines, purrs, and growls.

   The delicate kit fox is a pale-gray- to rust-colored fox with white fur
from belly to throat, a black tail tip, and proportionally larger ears
than its cousin, the gray fox. It is primarily a nocturnal animal, usually remaining in a burrow, often an enlarged marmot or badger den,
during the day. The kit fox swims well, and will climb trees in its
search for food. It is a territorial and solitary fox, so you can expect to
find the tracks of the same fox repeatedly in a given area.
   Little else is known about this shy little fox; its tracks are typically
canine, with four toe and nail prints usually visible. If you find several sets of tracks this size in the late summer, you might suspect a
family of young gray foxes out on a training hunt; but a single line of
tracks this size in remote areas is clear evidence of a kit fox's passage.

Kit Fox
life size in mud

GRAY FOX   *Urocyon cinereoargenteus*

Order: Carnivora (flesh-eating mammals). **Family:** Canidae (dogs).
Range and habitat: throughout Southern California; in chaparral and
brushy, sparsely wooded country. **Size and weight:** 40-42 inches; 12-
15 pounds. **Diet:** omnivorous, including small mammals, birds,
insects, eggs, fruit, nuts, grains, and other forage. **Sounds:** normally
silent, occasionally short barking yips.

This pretty fox with gray back, rusty flanks, and white underside is
generally nocturnal and secretive, but you might spot one foraging by
daylight in thick foliage or forested areas. The only canine in America
with the ability to climb, it frequently seeks refuge and food in trees,
but cottontails are the mainstay of its diet when they are available.
The gray fox typically dens among boulders on the slopes of rocky
ridges or in rock piles, hollow logs, or the like; it uses these dens in
winter as well as summer.

Gray fox tracks are usually distinct due to the relative lack of fur on
the animal's feet. The tracks always show the imprints of claws, with
7 to 12 inches between walking prints.

Gray Fox
life size in mud

59

BOBCAT
Wildcat

Felis rufus

Order: Carnivora (flesh-eating mammals). **Family:** Felidae (cats). **Range and habitat:** throughout Southern California; in forested foothills, swamps, and fringes, rimrock, and chaparral. **Size and weight:** 30 inches; 35 pounds. **Diet:** small mammals and birds; rarely carrion. **Sounds:** capable of generic cat-family range of noises.

The bobcat is a very adaptable feline, afield both day and night and wandering as far as 50 miles in a day of hunting, occasionally into suburban areas. It is primarily a ground hunter, but will climb trees and drop onto unsuspecting prey if the opportunity presents itself. You could mistake it for a large tabby cat with a bobbed tail, but the similarity ends there, for the bobcat has quite a wild disposition combined with greater size, strength, and razor-sharp claws and teeth.

You can expect to encounter bobcat tracks almost anywhere. You'll know the roundish tracks belong to a cat because the retractile claws never leave imprints and the toes usually spread a bit more than a dog's. Bobcat tracks are too large to be mistaken for those of a domestic cat, however. The animal's weight will have set the tracks deeper in a soft surface than you would expect from a house cat, and domestic cats have pads that are single-lobed at the front end. Bobcat tracks are clearly smaller than those of a mountain lion and are therefore easily identifiable by process of elimination.

Bobcat
life size in mud

61

VIRGINIA OPOSSUM   *Didelphis virginiana*

Order: Marsupialia (pouched mammals). **Family:** Didelphiidae. **Range and habitat:** most parts of Southern California; in woodlands and adjoining areas, and farmlands, generally remaining near streams and lakes; also common around human habitations. **Size and weight:** 25 inches; 12 pounds. **Diet:** this opportunistic omnivore prefers fruits, vegetables, insects, small mammals, birds, eggs, carrion; also garbage and pet food. **Sounds:** a gurgling hiss when annoyed.

The usually nocturnal opossum appears fairly ordinary: it looks like a large, long-haired rat, with pointed nose, pale-gray fur, and a long, scaly, reptilian tail. Primarily terrestrial, the opossum may nest in an abandoned burrow or a fallen tree, but will climb to escape danger. Other than climbing, its only defense mechanism is the ability to feign death, or "play possum."

In many respects, however, the opossum is the most peculiar animal residing on this continent. Among the oldest and most primitive of all living mammals, it is the only animal in North America with a prehensile (grasping) tail, the only nonprimate in the animal kingdom with an opposable (thumblike) digit (the inside toes on the hind feet), and the only marsupial on the continent. As many as fourteen young are born prematurely after only thirteen days of gestation, weighing only 1/15 of an ounce each (the whole litter would fit in a teaspoon!). The tiny babies crawl into their mother's pouch, where they remain for the next two months. After emerging from the pouch, they often ride around on the mother's back for some time. All of this pretty unusual behavior, even in Southern California.

Opossums leave easily identifiable tracks: the opposable hind thumb usually points 90 degrees or more away from the direction of travel, and the five toes spread widely. Like raccoons, opossums leave tracks in a row of pairs. Each pair consists of one front- and one rear-foot imprint, always close to or slightly overlapping each other, and the pairs are from 5 to 11 inches apart, depending on size and speed. The opossum's long tail frequently leaves drag marks on soft surfaces.

Virginia Opossum
life size in mud

COYOTE   *Canis latrans*
Brush wolf, prairie wolf

Order: Carnivora (flesh-eating mammals). **Family:** Canidae (dogs).
Range and habitat: widespread throughout Southern California; primarily in prairies, open woodlands, and brushy fringes, but very adaptable; can turn up anywhere. **Size and weight:** 48 inches; 45 pounds. **Diet:** omnivorous, including rodents and other small mammals, fish, carrion, insects, berries, grains, nuts, and vegetation. **Sounds:** wide range of canine sounds; most often heard yelping in group chorus late at night.

An important controller of small rodents, the smart, adaptable coyote is—unlike the gray wolf—steadily expanding its range. About the size of a collie, the coyote is a good runner and swimmer and has great stamina. Despite its wide range, it is shy, and you will be lucky to see one in the wild.

Typically canine, the coyote's front paw is slightly larger than the rear, and the front toes tend to spread wider, though not as wide as the bobcat's. The toenails nearly always leave imprints. The shape of coyote pads is unique, the front pads differing markedly from the rear, as shown, and the outer toes are usually slightly larger than the inner toes on each foot. The coyote tends to walk in a straight line and keep its tail down, which often leaves an imprint in deep snow. These characteristics plus walking strides of 8 to 16 inches and leaps to 10 feet may help you distinguish coyote tracks from those of domestic dogs with feet of the same size.

Coyote
life size in mud

RACCOON   *Procyon lotor*

Order: Carnivora (flesh-eating mammals). **Family:** Procyonidae (raccoons, ringtails, and coatis). **Range and habitat:** throughout Southern California; varied, mostly in forest fringe and rocky areas near streams, ponds, and lakes. **Size and weight:** 36 inches; 25 pounds. **Diet:** omnivorous, including fish, amphibians, shellfish, insects, birds, eggs, mice, carrion, berries, nuts, and vegetation. **Sounds:** a variety of shrill cries, whistles, churrs, growls, and screeches.

From childhood most of us know the raccoon by its mask of black fur and its black tail stripes on an otherwise grayish-brown body. It's familiar as a character in kids' books and frontier lore, frequently seen as a road kill, and is both curious and bold enough to be a fairly common visitor to campgrounds and even residential homes nearly everywhere within its range. Chiefly nocturnal, raccoons are more commonly sighted in suburban neighborhoods, raiding garbage cans and terrorizing family hounds, than in wildlands. Interesting and intelligent animals with manual dexterity of great renown, raccoons are also reputed to make lively and intriguing pets, provided they are closely supervised.

Raccoons like to wash or tear food items apart in water, which apparently improves their manual sensitivity. Much of their food comes from aquatic prospecting, so you will often find their tracks near water. When a raccoon walks, its left rear foot is placed next to the right front foot, and so forth, forming paired track clusters. Running-track clusters tend to be bunched irregularly. The walking stride of a raccoon is about 7 inches; leaps average 20 inches.

The ringtail, which lives in rocky habitats around most of the region, could be mistaken for a raccoon at a quick glimpse. The ringtail's body is more foxlike, its face has white eye rings rather than a black mask, and its tail has black *and white* stripes. Interestingly, its tracks resemble weasel-family tracks without claw prints, rather than those of its raccoon relatives.

Raccoon
life size in mud

DESERT COTTONTAIL   *Sylvilagus audubonii*

Order: Lagomorpha (rabbitlike mammals). **Family:** Leporidae (hares and rabbits). **Range and habitat:** throughout Southern California; in grasslands, creosote brush, and desert. **Size and weight:** 13 inches; 3 pounds. **Diet:** green vegetation, bark, twigs, sagebrush, and juniper berries. **Sounds:** usually silent; loud squeal when extremely distressed.

Cottontails are the pudgy, adorable rabbits with cottonball tails, known to us all from childhood tales of Peter Rabbit. Active day and night, year round, they're generally plentiful due in part to the fact that each adult female produces three or four litters of four to seven young rabbits each year. Of course, a variety of predators helps control their number, and few live more than a year in the wild.

Cottontail tracks are easily recognized because the basic pattern doesn't vary much, regardless of the rabbit's speed. It's important to note that, as with all rabbit-family tracks, sometimes the front feet land together, side by side, but just as often the second forefoot lands in line ahead of the first. The desert cottontail leaves track clusters that span 6 and 9 inches normally, with up to 3 feet between running clusters.

Of the two species of cottontail rabbits found in Southern California, the desert cottontail is the more widespread and abundant. The slightly smaller brush rabbit lives in coastal brushy areas.

You will have no problem telling cottontail tracks from those of jackrabbits, whose track clusters span as much as two feet, with up to 20 feet separating clusters; and because jackrabbits tend to run up on the toes of their hind feet, they often leave *smaller* hind foot imprints than cottontails do.

Desert Cottontail
life size in sand

PORCUPINE   *Erethizon dorsatum*
Porky, Quill Pig

   Order: Rodentia (gnawing mammals). **Family:** Erethizontidae (porcupines). **Range and habitat:** Angeles and San Bernardino national forests; usually in forested areas, also in brushy fringes, fields, meadows, and semidesert areas; a very adaptable animal. **Size and weight:** 30 inches; 25 pounds. **Diet:** vegetarian, including bark, leaves, fruits, berries, nuts, flowers. **Sounds:** normally quiet; capable of a great variety of grunts, whines, and harmonicalike noises and rapid teeth clicking.

   The porcupine is one of the few animals whose tracks you can follow with reasonable expectation of catching up with their maker. Often out during daylight hours, it moves quite slowly if not alarmed, stops frequently to nibble at vegetation, and does not see well; so if you're quiet, you can usually observe this peaceable animal at your and its leisure. An alarmed porcupine climbs a tree to escape danger, only using its quills as a last-ditch defense against an outright attack; and the porcupine cannot fling its quills, so there's no danger to any creature with enough sense to stay out of direct contact, a requisite that regrettably excludes many domestic dogs.
   Often the porcupine's distinctive shuffling gait and dragging whisk-broom tail may be the only clear track signs it leaves behind, especially in snow. In winter, porcupine trails often lead to or away from a coniferous tree, where the animal both sleeps and dines on bark and needles; alternatively, it may hole up in a den beneath a stump or in another ground-level shelter. Occasionally a piece of snow or mud that has stuck to a porcupine's foot will dislodge intact, revealing the unique pebbled texture of its soles. Imprints from the long claws are also often visible.

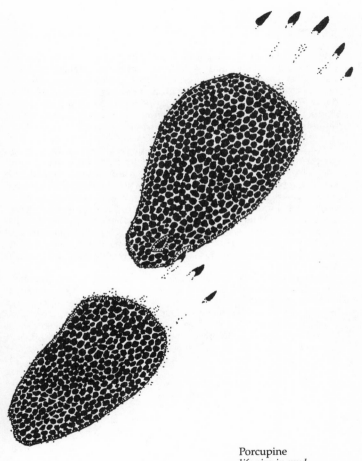

Porcupine
life size in mud

BADGER   *Taxidea taxus*

Order: Carnivora (flesh-eating mammals). **Family:** Mustelidae (the weasel family). **Range and habitat:** widespread throughout Southern California; in treeless meadows, semiopen prairies, grasslands, and deserts at all altitudes, wherever ground-dwelling rodents are abundant. **Size and weight:** 28 inches; 20 pounds. **Diet:** carnivorous, including all small rodents, snakes, birds, eggs, insects, and carrion. **Sounds:** may snarl or hiss when alarmed or annoyed.

The badger is a solitary creature that digs up most of its food and tunnels into the earth to escape danger. Its powerful short legs and long, strong claws are well suited to its earthmoving ways, and badgers can reputedly dig faster than a man with a shovel. Above ground the badger is a fierce fighter threatened only by much larger carnivores. The animal is active in daylight and not too shy, even entering campgrounds in its search for food. Its facial markings are quite distinctive and easily recognized: the face is black with white ears and cheeks and a white stripe running from its nose over the top of its head. The rest of the body is light brown or gray, and the feet are black.

Badger tracks show five long, clear toe prints of each foot and obvious marks left by the long front claws. The animal walks on its soles, which may or may not leave complete prints. Its pigeon-toed trail may be confused with the porcupine's in deep snow, but a porcupine trail will invariably lead to a tree or into a natural den, a badger's to a burrow of its own excavation. Another clue: the badger's short, soft tail rarely leaves a mark.

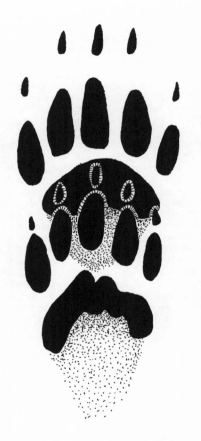

Badger
life size in mud

73

PRONGHORN   *Antilocapra americana*
Antelope

Order: Artiodactyla (even-toed hoofed mammals). **Family:** Antilocapridae (pronghorns). **Range and habitat:** east of San Bernardino; on open prairies and sagebrush plains. **Height and weight:** 36 inches at shoulder; 120 pounds. **Diet:** vegetation, including weeds, shrubs, grasses, and herbs; fond of sagebrush. **Sounds:** usually silent, but capable of a loud whistling sound when startled.

The pronghorn is the most easily observed of Southern Californian hoofed mammals. This sociable animal lives in flat, open country, and its tan hide marked with striking rump patches, white underside, and facial spots is easy to recognize. The fastest animals in North America, pronghorns race around en masse at speeds of 45 miles per hour or so.

Because the pronghorn is easily sighted from a distance, you normally won't have to rely on tracks for identification, but the tracks should be easy to recognize because, unlike the mule deer, which shares much of its range, the pronghorn has no dewclaws. It is more gregarious than deer, and its running characteristics are unique: a large group of pronghorns may run for a mile or more in a straight line, whereas deer tend to run only when startled and then they don't run very far. The pronghorn's great speed produces an average separation of 14 feet between track clusters; running white-tailed deer average 6 feet, and mule deer average about 10 feet.

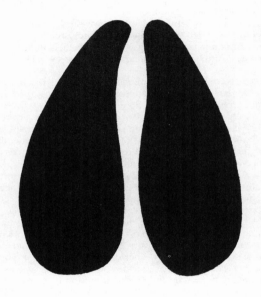

Pronghorn
life size in mud

WILD BOAR   *Sus scrofa*

Order: Artiodactyla (even-toed hoofed mammals). **Family:** Suidae.
Range and habitat: Los Padres National Forest; habitat variable, including dense forests, adjoining brushlands, dry hills, and swampy
fringes, particularly in winter. **Height and weight:** 36 inches at shoulder; 300 pounds. **Diet:** acorns and other nuts, roots, grasses, fruit,
also small amphibians, eggs, occasionally small mammals and carrion. **Sounds:** grunts and squeals typical of domestic pigs.

Wild boars were brought from Europe in 1925 to stock hunting pre-
serves in Monterey County, where some inevitably escaped and bred
with feral domestic pigs; today, Southern California's wild boars are
almost entirely hybrids. These brown or gray creatures are recognizably piglike in shape, but their humped backs, shaggy coats, and formidable tusks readily distinguish them from domestic animals.
Strong, agile, and occasionally aggressive, wild boars can be dangerous to encounter in the dense vegetation they tend to prefer. They are
most active at dawn and dusk, are good swimmers and fast runners,
and usually move about in family groups of six or so animals, occasionally congregating in herds of up to fifty.

The cloven tracks of wild boars could be mistaken for those of mule
deer, which overlap their range, but note that wild boar tracks are
more rounded, with toes more splayed, heels together—often to the
extent that no break is apparent in the imprint at all—and dewclaw
imprints, in soft ground, are farther out to the sides than you'd find
in deer tracks. Wild boars have strides of about 18 inches, usually in
a narrow line; they root around on the ground in their search for nuts
and other food, leaving behind characteristic diggings, and rub or
gouge trees with their tusks within 3 feet of the ground. Mule deer,
on the other hand, leave narrower hoofprints with heels usually sep-
arated, 24-inch strides, and evidence of browsing in foliage 5 or 6 feet
above the ground.

Wild Boar
life size in mud

MULE DEER

Odocoileus hemionus

Order: Artiodactyla (even-toed hoofed mammals). **Family:** Cervidae (deer). **Range and habitat:** widespread throughout Southern California; in mixed forests and adjoining areas at all elevations, regularly moving into grasslands, chaparral, and desert fringes that have browse plants available. **Height and weight:** 42 inches at shoulder; 350 pounds. **Diet:** herbivorous, including leaves, grasses, grains, nuts, and berries. **Sounds:** generally silent, but produces a snorting whistle when alarmed; makes occasional grunts and other vocal noises.

The mule deer is easily recognized by its large ears and black-tipped tail, which it holds down when running. Active during the day and at dusk, the mule deer can be observed fairly often in the wild. Skittish, at the first sign of alarm it flees with a unique feet-together bounding gait, all four hooves landing and taking off at the same time. This gait is an adaptation to life in rugged, often densely brushy terrain. The mule deer is also a strong swimmer.

Mule deer tracks show small, slender hooves usually spread slightly at the heels and, often, dewclaw impressions. The doubled-over walking tracks are usually less than 2 feet apart; at speeds beyond a walk, the mule deer bounds, leaving very distinctive clusters of parallel tracks 10 feet or more apart.

Mule Deer
life size in mud

BIGHORN SHEEP
Desert bighorn, mountain sheep

Ovis canadensis

Order: Artiodactyla (even-toed hoofed mammals). **Family:** Bovidae (cattle, sheep, and goats). **Range and habitat:** eastern two-thirds of Southern California; in mountainous, sparsely populated terrain and high, hilly desert, avoiding forested areas. **Height and weight:** 45 inches at shoulder; 275 pounds. **Diet:** variety of high-altitude browse, grasses, herbs, lichens. **Sounds:** loudest and most recognizable are the sounds of head and horn butting made by competing rams during late fall; coughs, grunts, bleating.

This big sheep, with its distinctive white rump and heavy coiled horns, lives in remote areas of southeastern California, where its hooves with their hard outer edges and spongy centers give it excellent agility on rocky surfaces. It tends, however, to prefer high mountain meadows and scree slopes. In the summer, you commonly see groups of about ten ewes and lambs grazing or lying around chewing their cuds. In winter, rams join the herd, which may grow in size to 100 animals or more. The most distinctive behavior of the bighorn sheep is the frenzied, high-speed head butting engaged in by competing rams before the autumn mating season; noise from the impact carries a great distance in the open mountain country. Thanks to nature documentaries shown on television, people have had the opportunity to witness this head-butting ritual without having to venture into remote mountainous wildlands, thus saving wear and tear on fragile ecosystems and human knee joints.

Because of the habitat where they are commonly found, bighorn sheep tracks are rarely confused with those of other hoofed animals. The hooves average 3½ inches in length, longer than those of deer but not as big as those of elk. Rather blunt and square, the hooves may show signs of wear and tear from the scree slopes; dewclaw prints are never left.

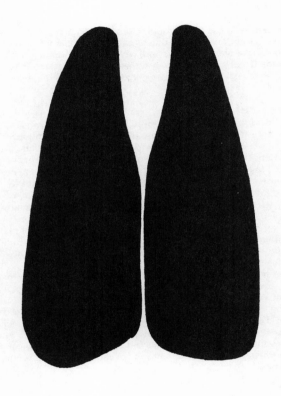

Bighorn Sheep
life size in mud

BISON
Buffalo

Bison bison

Order: Artiodactyla (even-toed hoofed mammals). **Family:** Bovidae (cattle, sheep, and goats). **Range and habitat:** Santa Catalina Island; on open grassland. **Height and weight:** 72 inches at shoulder; 2000 pounds. **Diet:** grazes mostly on grass; occasionally browses for buds, bark, twigs, shoots, and other vegetation. **Sounds:** a range of bovine noises.

Their dark brown, shaggy mane and beard, massive humped shoulders, and sharp, stout, upturned horns make Great Plains bison unmistakable. In 1880 more than 40 million bison grazed peacefully and stolidly in America, seldom taking notice of humans. Today there are 100,000 bison in the United States, largely captive and controlled in ten major public herds and many smaller private ones.

Fourteen bison were brought to Santa Catalina Island in 1924 for the filming of Zane Grey's novel *The Vanishing American*. The film crew left the animals behind when they departed. The gene pool was supplemented in 1934 with the addition of 30 animals from Colorado, and again in the 1970s with animals from Montana. Today Santa Catalina Island has the only free-roaming herd of bison in Southern California, the herd size being maintained between at 400 and 500 head.

Bison are quite gregarious animals. It's a mistake to read meekness into the bison's seemingly mild-mannered indifference, however, because bison are huge and quick, quick enough to outrun a horse over a ¼-mile course. It's a good idea to treat a bison with the same respect and common sense you would any large, domestic bull.

Bison tracks are a unique shape and size, measuring roughly 5 inches in each direction, with about 25 to 30 inches between walking track clusters. Bison also like to roll around, forming prominent dust wallows.

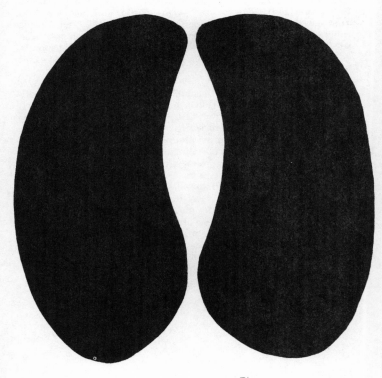

Bison
life size in mud

MOUNTAIN LION
Puma, cougar, panther, catamount

Felis concolor

Order: Carnivora (flesh-eating mammals). **Family:** Felidae (cats). **Range and habitat:** Los Padres National Forest, and Colorado River drainage; in rugged wilderness mountains, forests, and swamp fringes. **Size and weight:** 84 inches; 200 pounds. **Diet:** primarily deer, small mammals, and birds; occasionally domestic animals. **Sounds:** generally quiet, but capable of a variety of loud feline screams, hisses, and growls.

Hunted to the verge of extinction, our large, tawny, native American cat with its long, waving tail is now so scarce and secretive and is confined to such remote terrain that you'd be very lucky to sight one in the wild. But you at least have a chance to find the tracks of this big cat, which hunts mostly on the ground. It occasionally climbs trees, particularly to evade dogs but also to drop onto unwary prey (the mountain lion acts as an important natural control over the deer population).

Because of their size, mountain lion tracks can't normally be confused with any others. Spacing of tracks will also be what you'd expect of the large cat: trail width of 12 inches or more, walking tracks over 20 inches apart, 3 feet separating pairs of loping tracks, and bounding leaps of 12 feet or more. Also look for tail-drag marks, especially in snow. Of course, like most cats, the mountain lion has retractile claws, which never leave marks.

Mountain Lion
life size in mud

BLACK-TAILED JACKRABBIT
Lepus californicus
Jackass rabbit

Order: Lagomorpha (rabbitlike mammals). **Family:** Leporidae (hares and rabbits). **Range and habitat:** throughout Southern California; in open prairies and sparsely vegetated sage and cactus country. **Size and weight:** 20 inches; 6 pounds. **Diet:** mostly grasses and other green vegetation, often along highway edges; also shrubs, buds, bark, twigs, and cultivated crops. **Sounds:** normally silent.

The black-tailed jackrabbit, the most widespread and numerous jackrabbit of Southern California, is easily recognized by its year-round light-gray fur, white underside, and distinctive black fur patch on top of the tail. It is most active from dusk to dawn and spends most of its days lying in depressions it scoops out at the base of a bush, by a rock, or at any other spot that gives it a bit of protection. These jackrabbits are sociable and are often seen feeding in small groups.

Front prints, about 3 inches long, are usually compact but often splayed, as shown; are usually the same size regardless of speed, and fall behind in the rear, a pattern typical of all rabbits. Hind prints vary greatly in size. Walking slowly and flat-footed, jackrabbits leave narrow rear prints about 6 inches long, but as speed increases, its heels lift until, at top speed of 35 to 40 miles per hour, only the toes leave prints, about 3½ inches long, sometimes resembling coyote tracks.

The most distinguishing track characteristic of jackrabbits, however, is that at running speed they leap repeatedly from 7 to 12 feet and more. Coyotes rarely leap more than 6 feet, and cottontails bound no more than 3 feet.

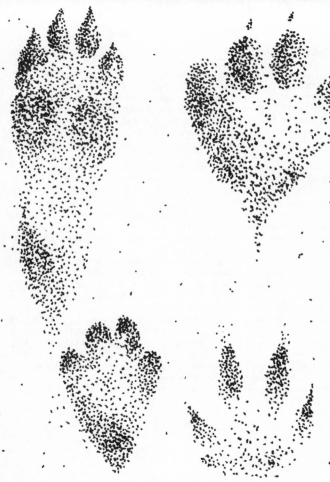

Black-tailed Jackrabbit
½ life size in sand

BEAVER   *Castor canadensis*

Order: Rodentia (gnawing mammals). **Family:** Castoridae (beavers). **Range and habitat:** from Colorado River west to Palm Springs, south to Mexico; in streams and lakes with brush and trees or in open forest along riverbanks. **Size and weight:** 36 inches; 55 pounds. **Diet:** aquatic plants, bark, and the twigs and leaves of many shrubs and trees, preferably alder, cottonwood, and willow. **Sounds:** nonvocal, but smacks tail on water surface quite loudly to signal danger.

Thia industrious aquatic mammal is the largest North American rodent. Although it sometimes lives unobtrusively in a riverbank, usually it constructs the familiar beaver lodge, a roughly conical pile of brush, stones, and mud extending as much as 6 feet above the surface of a pond, and gnaws down dozens of small softwood trees with which it constructs a conspicuous system of dams, often several hundred yards long. A beaver can grasp objects with its front paws and stand and walk upright on its hind feet. It uses its flat, scaly, strong tail for support out of water and as a rudder when swimming. Gregarious animals, beavers work well together on their collective projects. They are active day and night year round, but may operate unobserved beneath the ice (wherever present) during much of the winter, using subsurface lodge entrances.

If you are lucky, the large, webbed hind-foot tracks left by a beaver will be clear, with 6 to 8 inches between pairs. Beavers frequently, however, obscure part or most of their tracks by dragging their tails and/or branches over them, leaving a trail much like that of a 6-inch-wide turtle, except that the beaver's tail-drag trail zigzags slightly every 6 or 8 inches. The zigzag is the key to identification; a turtle moves in reasonably long, straight segments until it changes direction significantly.

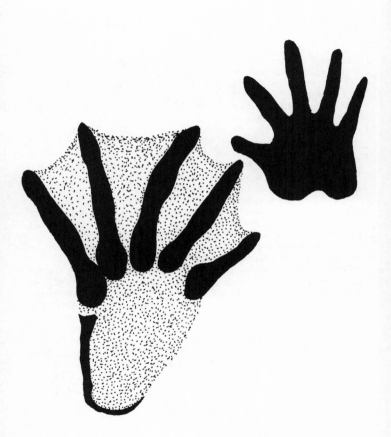

Beaver
½ life size in mud

BLACK BEAR   *Ursus americanus*
Cinnamon bear

Order: Carnivora (flesh-eating mammals). **Family:** Ursidae (bears).
Range and habitat: Los Padres National Forest; primarily in medium-to-higher-elevation mountainous forests and swamp fringes. **Size and weight:** 6½ feet; 450 pounds. **Diet:** omnivorous, including smaller mammals, fish, carrion, insects, fruit, berries, nuts, and succulent plants. **Sounds:** usually silent, but may growl, grunt, woof, whimper or make other immediately recognizable indications of annoyance or alarm.

The black bear is the smallest and most common American bear. You may have seen these animals around rural garbage dumps and in parks. In the wild, it is shy and wary of human contact as a general rule and thus not frequently sighted. If you do sight one, however, it can be very dangerous to underestimate it. The black bear is very strong, agile, and quick. It climbs trees, swims well, can run 25 miles per hour for short stretches, and above all else, is unpredictable; it may seem docile and harmless in parks, but it has been known to chase people with great determination.

Be alert for bear trails, worn deep by generations of bears, and for trees with claw marks and other indications of bear territory. Bear tracks are usually easy to identify; they are roughly human in shape and size but slightly wider. The large claws leave prints wherever the toes do. If a bear slips on mud or ice, its soles leave distinctive smooth slide marks; nearby you will no doubt find more orderly tracks. Both adult black and immature grizzly bear tracks measure about 7 inches in length, but the grizzly bear (shown on California's state flag) was exterminated in the state in the 1920s.

Black Bear   91
½ *life size in mud*

SEA OTTER   *Enhydra lutris*

Order: Carnivora (flesh-eating mammals). **Family:** Mustelidae (weasels and skunks). **Range and habitat:** Channel Islands, and coastal waters from Point Conception north; salt water only. **Size and weight:** 40 inches; 40 pounds. **Diet:** mollusks, crabs, other shellfish, fish, other marine animals. **Sounds:** hisses loudly when alarmed.

The sea otter is an agile and energetic ocean-living otter that has lived along the west coast of America since the Ice Age. Its real troubles began when its fur became the royal fur of China; in the first half of the nineteenth century, Russian and Aleut fur hunters nearly exterminated the animals. Since 1911, sea otters have been protected by a variety of international treaties and U.S. federal laws, and their numbers and range are now expanding.

Sea otters are born buoyant as corks, learn to swim quickly, and spend their lives inconspicuously among offshore rocks or patches of floating vegetation. They are among the few species of tool-using mammals worldwide; you might occasionally hear or observe a sea otter floating on its back and breaking a shellfish open with a stone brought up from the bottom expressly for that purpose. Apart from their wild habitalts, sea otters can be observed at several fine aquariums in Southern California.

Sea otters don't come ashore very often, but when they do, they leave the only readily identifiable tracks of all the sea mammals that visit Southern California's shores, primarily six species of true and eared seals.

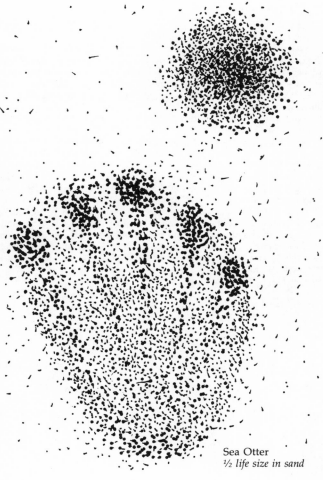

Sea Otter
½ life size in sand

93

SEA TURTLES
Order: Chelonia

Four species of ocean-dwelling turtles occasionally visit the waters and beaches of Southern California during warm summer months: the hawksbill, loggerhead, green (all of the Chelonidae family), and leatherback (of the Dermochelyidae family), which, with a maximum shell diameter of 7 feet, is the largest living turtle and the most specialized turtle, with a smooth leathery skin instead of the normal rigid turtle shell.

Regrettably, these great turtles are probably destined to become extinct within the next couple of decades. Few hatchlings survive to maturity; adults fall prey to a variety of difficulties (including drowning in commercial fishing nets); the animals require up to thirty years to reach sexual maturity; and development of coastal real estate continues to encroach on potential nesting sites.

Because they have clawless, paddlelike flippers, sea turtles leave easily identifiable trails of grooves alternating alongside a drag path of shell width. In most cases you can identify the species that made the track simply by measuring the width of the shell-drag trail: hawksbill to 36 inches, loggerhead to 48, green to 60, and leatherback to 80 inches or more.

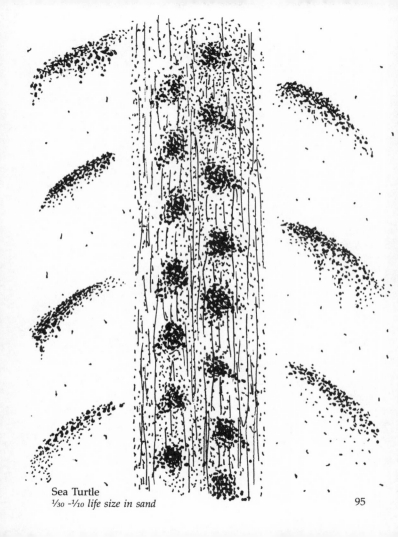

Sea Turtle
1/30 - 1/10 life size in sand

Birds

HORNED LARK
Eremophila alpestris

Order: Passeriformes (perching birds). **Family:** Alaudidae (larks). **Range and habitat:** year-round residents throughout Southern California; in large fields, open areas, shorelines; especially in winter in large, freshly manured fields. **Size and weight:** wingspan 8 inches; a few ounces. **Diet:** insects and seeds. **Sounds:** a weak, high-pitched song, repeated many times while in flight high overhead; winter call consists of faint tinkling notes.

The horned lark is a small, ground-feeding bird easily recognized by its black face and neck bands and small black feathered tufts above the eyes. This bird usually walks, and if alarmed, usually returns to the ground after a short flight. Because of the uniquely lengthy rear toe of the horned lark, it is, under normal circumstances, the only species of small perching land birds whose tracks can be differentiated. If you find tracks, either walking or hopping, of similar size but in which the single rear toe is not much longer than any of the front three, you will know that you have found the tracks of any one of various small land birds that either reside in or visit Southern California, including dippers, chickadees, mockingbirds, thrushes, pipits, starlings, juncos, or one of about seventeen species of sparrow; these are the Passeriformes that spend any appreciable amount of time on the ground leaving tracks.

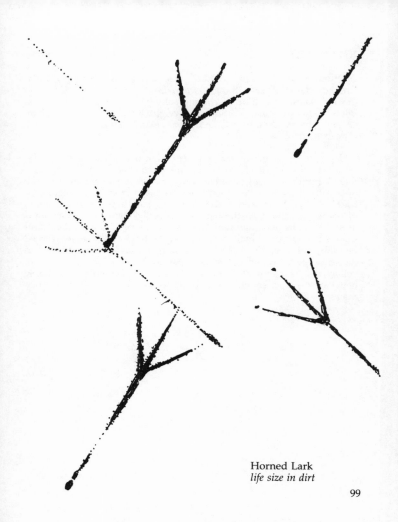

Horned Lark
life size in dirt

KILLDEER

Charadrius vociferus

Order: Charadriiformes (shorebirds, gulls, and terns). **Family:** Charadriidae (plovers). **Range and habitat:** year-round resident in most of Southern California; common along shorelines, also found on inland fields and pastures. **Size and weight:** 8 inches, wingspan 12 inches; 4 ounces. **Diet:** insects and larvae, earthworms, seeds. **Sounds:** repeats its name as its call.

The killdeer is one of the most common and recognizable shorebirds. Its two black breast bands are distinctive, as is its habit of feigning injury to lead intruders away from its nesting area. The killdeer is the only shorebird found year round in most of the region. Its tracks are typical as well of the tracks—usually found in deep sand—of shorebirds that visit the region seasonally: the front center toe is longer than the two outer toes; the small hind toe, more of a heel spur than a toe, leaves a small imprint; and the tracks are usually printed in a line, only 1 or 2 inches apart for birds the size of the killdeer, less for sandpipers, and up to 6 inches apart for birds the size of a greater yellowlegs. The general shape and lack of any evidence of webbing between the toes separate shorebird tracks from those of gulls or ducks.

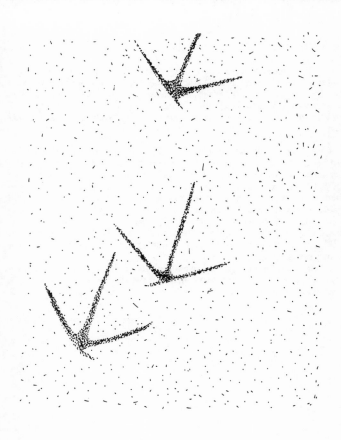

Killdeer
life size in sand

AMERICAN CROW   *Corvus brachyrhynchos*

Order: Passeriformes (perching birds). **Family:** Corvidae (jays, magpies, crows). **Range and habitat:** year-round resident throughout Southern California; in all habitats except extremely arid regions. **Size and weight:** length 17 inches, wingspan 26 inches; 1 pound. **Diet:** nearly everything from mice to carrion to garbage. **Sounds:** distinctive "caw."

Crows are relatively intelligent birds, quite vocal, make good pets, and can be taught to mimic human voices. Researchers have also determined that crows can count, and both wild and pet crows have been observed making up games to play. Watching crows will often help you locate other wildlife, too: groups of crows will mob and scold a predator such as an owl, for example, or perch near an offensive animal, darting in to harass and scold it. The common crow can be told from a distant hawk by its frequent steady flapping; it seldom glides more than two or three seconds except in strong updrafts or when descending.

All four of the crow's toes are about the same length, each with a strong claw, all of which leave prints most of the time. Crows walk and skip; their tracks are not usually made in pairs.

American Crow
life size in mud

103

NORTHERN FLICKER

Colaptes auratus

Order: Piciformes (woodpeckers and allies). **Family:** Picidae. **Range and habitat:** year-round resident throughout Southern California; in open country near large trees. **Size and weight:** length, 10 inches, wingspan, 14 inches; weight, 4 ounces. **Diet:** insects. **Sounds:** loud repeated flick or flicker, also shrill descending "kee-oo."

Widespread and common, the flicker is most easily recognized by the black polka-dots on its white chest and belly, and the yellow or orange plumage under its wings. These jay-sized woodpeckers often fly down to the ground to eat ants and other insects and grubs.

A variety of other woodpeckers and the yellow-bellied sapsucker visit or reside in Southern California; all have feet of the same distinctive shape, adapted for clinging to tree trunks and limbs while the birds dig for wood-boring insects; but they rarely leave the trees, so when you find tracks like those illustrated, you can feel reasonably sure they were left by a ground-visiting flicker.

Northern Flicker
life size in mud

CALIFORNIA QUAIL   *Callipepla californica*

Order: Galliformes (terrestrial birds). **Family:** Phasianidae (turkeys, grouse, and quail). **Range and habitat:** year-round resident throughout Southern California; common in mixed woodlands and in large city parks. **Size and weight:** length 5 inches, wingspan 12 inches; 8 ounces. **Diet:** seeds and insects. **Sounds:** calls with three slurred notes, the middle one highest and loudest.

This small, plump quail with prominent black teardrop topknot extending a couple of inches above its forehead is usually seen in small flocks feeding on the ground. Typical of the Galliformes, if alarmed it will fly a short distance with very rapid wingbeats before returning to earth. All of the birds in this family spend most of their lives on the ground. They run nearly everywhere, and their feet have evolved for this lifestyle; the very small hind toe, used only occasionally for balance when the bird is standing still, rarely touches the ground. Thus, the track of the California quail is representative of, and identical in shape to, the other Galliformes that reside year round in various parts of Southern California, including the wild turkey, blue grouse, mountain quail, and the introduced chukar and ring-necked pheasants. Track size will vary according to individual species.

California Quail
life size in mud

107

CINNAMON TEAL
Anas cyanoptera

Order: Anseriformes. **Family:** Anatidae (waterfowl). **Range and habitat:** year-round resident of Southern California; in ponds, marshes, protected bays, and marinas. **Size and weight:** length 17 inches, wingspan 25 inches; 1 pound. **Diet:** small aquatic animals and vegetation. **Sounds:** male peeps, female quacks softly.

The cinnamon teal is a common, shy, surface-feeding duck that you will see flying rapidly in small, tight flocks. The male is easily identified by his cinnamon-red head and underparts; the female has a grayish-brown back, mottled light brown undersides, and white or pale-gray wing patches.

The cinnamon teal's tracks are identical in shape to those of all the aquatic waterfowl (ducks and geese) as well as the gulls, terns, and a variety of offshore seabirds residing year round or visiting Southern California seasonally. Track size, of course, will vary according to species.

Cinnamon Teal
life size in mud

BURROWING OWL   *Athene cuninularia*

Order: Strigiformes (owls). **Family:** Strigidae (all but barn owls).
Range and habitat: year-round resident throughout Southern California; plains and open, arid regions. **Size and weight:** length 6 inches, wingspan 22 inches; 1 pound. **Diet:** small mammals, mostly rodents. **Sounds:** a cackling alarm note and, at night, a two-note "coo-o-o."

Of the dozen or so species of owls that either reside year round or live seasonally in Southern California, the burrowing owl probably leaves more tracks than all others combined. This small, sandy-colored owl with a black throat band is active during the day, when you might observe it hovering while hunting above the open spaces it prefers; but more often it perches on fence posts or lands on the ground, where it bobs up and down on its proportionally long legs.

This owl nests underground, often locating a desert tortoise burrow or ground squirrel den and making further excavations to suit its needs. Its tracks are representative of all owl tracks, which will vary in size according to species, with those of the great horned owl being more than twice as large as those of the burrowing owl.

Burrowing Owl
life size in mud

ROADRUNNER

Geococcyx californianus

Order: Cuculiformes (cuckoos, anis, and roadrunners). **Family:** Cuculidae. **Range and habitat:** year-round resident throughout lower elevations of Southern California; in open, arid regions. **Size and weight:** length 22 inches, wingspan, 27 inches; 1 pound. **Diet:** lizards, snakes, insects, and spiders. **Sounds:** series of descending notes, dovelike.

Anyone who has spent a little time in the desert and/or watched a few old cartoons is familiar with the habits of this medium-sized, crested, mostly terrestrial bird, which dashes about so swiftly and purposefully, trailing its long white-tipped tail. One cannot help but sympathize with the coyote.

Roadrunner tracks are probably the most common and recognizable bird tracks found in the dry portions of the southwestern United States, and are unlikely to be confused with any other tracks, with 10 to 12 inches or more between distinctively shaped prints.

Roadrunner
life size in sand

TURKEY VULTURE
Cathartes aura

Order: Falconiformes (vultures, eagles, hawks, and falcons). **Family:** Cathartidae (vultures). **Range and habitat:** year-round resident throughout Southern California; commonly seen scavenging in fields and along roadsides nearly everywhere. **Size and weight:** wingspan to 6 feet; 3 pounds. **Diet:** carrion. **Sounds:** generally silent.

The turkey vulture is a large black bird that is easily recognized by its naked red head and neck (or naked gray face of immature birds), and by the two-toned wings that form a broad V as the bird soars in wide circles, looking for dead animals. Vultures are usually seen soaring in groups of several or many birds, and they will be joined by more as soon as they find something to eat; this is the characteristic that makes turkey vulture tracks easy to identify. A single track could be confused with that of an eagle or heron, but you will generally find hundreds of vulture tracks wherever you find any at all.

The track shape, however, with strong, thick toes and long, curved talons leaving significant prints, is representative of all the falcons, hawks, bald and golden eagles, and California condors that might be encountered in Southern California. None of the other Falconiformes congregate in large groups on the ground; in fact, most rarely come to earth at all. Track size will vary according to species, with those of the eagles being slightly larger, while most hawks and falcons have feet about half this size.

Turkey Vulture
life size in mud

GREAT BLUE HERON   *Ardea herodias*

Order: Ciconiiformes (herons and allies). **Family:** Ardeidae (herons, egrets, and bitterns). **Range and habitat:** throughout Southern California; in most lowland areas, common on fresh-water and ocean shores. **Size and weight:** length 48 inches, wingspan 72 inches; 7 pounds. **Diet:** fish, snakes, insects, mice, and frogs. **Sounds:** "kraak" and strident honks.

The presence of a great blue heron magically transforms an aquatic landscape, adding an aura of quiet elegance characteristic of the best Oriental brush paintings. This large heron typically walks slowly through shallows or stands with head hunched on shoulders, looking for the fish that make up a large part of its diet. A heron's nest, maintained year after year, is an elaborate structure of sticks 3 feet across built in a tree; great blue herons often nest colonially.

You will most often find great blue heron tracks bordering the fresh-water areas where the bird feeds. The four toes and claws of each foot usually leave visible imprints. The well-developed hind toe enables the heron to stand for long periods of time on one leg or the other or to walk very slowly while hunting.

This track shape is typical of all the herons, egrets, bitterns, and ibis found around the region at various times of year. The size and location of the tracks will vary according to species, but the offset front toe pattern distinguishes this group of wading birds from sandhill cranes, rails, and other shorebirds of Southern California.

Great Blue Heron
life size in mud

Recommended Reading

CARE OF THE WILD FEATHERED AND FURRED: A Guide to Wildlife Handling and Care, Mae Hickman and Maxine Guy (Unity Press, 1973); unique perspectives on animal behavior and emergency care of injured and orphaned wildlife.

A FIELD GUIDE TO ANIMAL TRACKS, second edition, Olaus J. Murie (Houghton Mifflin Co., Boston, 1975); a classic work on track identification by Murie (1889-1963), an eminent naturalist and wildlife artist; one of the Peterson Field Guide Series; an excellent research text for home study.

A FIELD GUIDE TO THE MAMMALS, third edition, W. H. Burt and R. P. Grossenheider (Houghton Mifflin Co., Boston, 1976); a good general field guide.

ISLAND SOJOURN, Elizabeth Arthur (Harper & Row, 1980); an account of life on an island in British Columbia's wilderness, with a chapter devoted to a metaphysical perspective of animal tracks.

SNOW TRACKS, Jean George (E. P. Dutton, 1958); an introduction to the study of animal tracks for very young children.

THE TRACKER, Tom Brown and William J. Watkins (Berkley Publications, 1984); an intriguing story by a man who has devoted his life to the science of following tracks and other movement clues of various animals, including humans.

Index

About the author:

Chris Stall first became interested in wild country and wild animals as a Boy Scout in rural New York State, where he spent his youth. In the two decades since, he has traveled and lived around most of North America, studying, photographing, sketching, and writing about wild animals in their natural habits. His photos and articles have appeared in a number of outdoor and nature magazines.